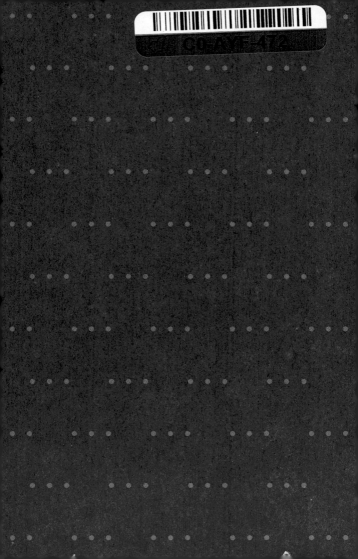

You Know You're a Writer When . . .

You Know You're a Writer When . . .

by Adair Lara

CHRONICLE BOOKS
SAN FRANCISCO

Library of Congress Cataloging-in-Publication Data available.

ISBN-10: 0-8118-6079-5
ISBN-13: 978-0-8118-6097-6

Manufactured in Canada

Designed by Brooke Johnson

Distributed in Canada by Raincoast Books
9050 Shaughnessy Street
Vancouver, British Columbia V6P 6E5

10 9 8 7 6 5 4 3 2 1

Chronicle Books LLC
680 Second Street
San Francisco, California 94107

www.chroniclebooks.com

This book is for my husband, Bill. You know you're a happily married writer when your best editor doubles as your husband.

Acknowledgments

I want to thank Chronicle Books for coming up with this great idea for a book and asking me to do it. Special thanks to my wonderful editor, Brianna Smith, and to the contributors: Stacy Appel, Joane Azevedo-Luesse, Robin Cruz, Gene Daly, Joan Frank, Rita Hargrave, Patrick Heig, Jan Jessel, Anne Kaiser, Linda Kilby, Bill LeBlond, Donna Levin, Nancy Murphy, Janis Newman, Margee Robinson, Marsh Rose, Barbara Saunders, Imma Trillo, John Trumble, Anne Wright, and Georgia Zweber.

Introduction

If you're a writer, chances are you'll recognize yourself in this book. You know that being a writer is not as simple as saying, duh, a writer is someone who writes. Writing is not a job, something you do. It's something you are, something you can't not be. Being a writer is not a matter of being published, or wearing sweaters with leather patches on the elbows, or smoking a pipe. It's about being so bewitched by language that writing seems real, and life by comparison feels like a dream.

How do you find out what being a writer means to those who really are writers? You ask them. Here is what the ink-stained, carpal-tunneled, slightly dazed, wordstruck people I know had to say.

"You Know You're a Writer When . . ."

You'll never forgive your parents for your happy childhood.

People still talk about your letters
from camp, or the navy, or jail.

You wonder if there's another word
for "thesaurus."

You know more than ten synonyms
for "blue."

The doctor tells you that you have terminal cancer and you think, "I can use this."

♂

Writing is the only thing you do that doesn't make you feel as if you should be doing something else.

A cop gives you a ticket and you realize
he's a sort of writer, too, and want to
say to him, "Can I just say your work
really has an impact on me?"

You want to commit suicide just so you
can break their hearts with the stoic
beauty of the note you leave.

You drink coffee black because Balzac did.

You are shipwrecked on a deserted island but can't send the rescue note off in the bottle because you have no access to spell-check.

You have an opinion on the serial comma.

You've switched to stretchier pants and looser sweaters to hide the effects of hours at the keyboard.

When driving alone on a stormy night past wind-tossed trees, you think, *She swerved to avoid the deer, but its hooves shattered the windshield into a cobweb of cracks, and then the car tumbled down the cliff. It rolled several times and came to rest at the bottom of the canyon. She was still alive.*

On your tombstone you would like these
words: "Whatever he accomplished or
failed to accomplish, it cannot be said
that the occupant suffered in silence."

You record any thoughts you deem pub-
lishable.

You have kept every letter you ever
received and copies of every letter
you've ever sent, for when you're
famous.

You put twigs in your pocket on your
walks to remind you of an idea to write
down when you get home.

You stop in the middle of
a fight with your husband—
"Hold on, honey!"—to jot
down a note.

Your pet peeve is people who use the word "literally" wrong—such as "I literally cooked each recipe in my head." Such errors make you see red—figuratively.

You know that stories about cats or the death penalty get the most mail from readers.

There are large containers of writing implements in all your rooms, like bouquets of flowers.

After your book is rejected, you fire
off a 4,000-word e-mail to your friends,
vowing never to write another word.

While working on a book, you are so
distracted that you miss your stop on
the bus and have to catch a bus back,
only to miss your stop again.

Your editor is either a genius or an
overpaid idiot, depending on what she
thinks of your work.

You're thinking about
moving to Europe so you'll
have something new to
write about.

One place you have in mind
is Ireland, where writers
are not taxed.

You circle a "C" for copyright on the
note you leave for the FedEx guy.

You take a tape recorder on visits home
to see your parents.

You think you should do the talk shows
first, sell the movie rights, and then, if
there's time, go back and write the book.

All you can do on your 500-gigabyte,
G-force, gazillion-feature computer is
type and save.

You get irritated at your girlfriend because she wants some hot lovin' and you want to write.

Every surface in your house has morphed into a desk: the kitchen island, the bed, the dining room table, the top of your antiquated television.

You can't wait for company to go the hell home.

You carry a canvas book bag from a writers' conference.

You get around to putting on your makeup an hour before bedtime.

You secretly love your own handwriting.

Your office is any café with an outlet.

Your son asks, "Mommy, are you ever going to have a job again?"

There are three empty cereal bowls next to your computer—one for each meal.

Something bad happens to a friend and
you're glad she's not a writer, so you
can use it.

All your bedspreads have ink stains
on them.

You go to bed at night and it's not your
own problems that keep you awake,
but those of your characters: *How will
Clarissa get her letters back before the wife
of her married lover publishes them in the
newspaper?*

You eat dinner with your plate on your knees because your manuscript is laid out on the table.

Your mother is writing her own book to set the record straight.

Your husband stops in the middle of lovemaking and says angrily, "Who's Sebastian?" and you realize that you called out your protagonist's name instead of his.

You accidentally sign a
check with your pen name.

You stop your friend in the midst of a story she's telling you to say, "Wouldn't it be better if you had your sister run off with the first-grade teacher instead of the hairdresser?"

You hide your journal on your lap at your kid's soccer game and rely on other moms to give you the answer to the "Guess how many goals I scored!" quiz at the end.

You own more than five pairs of sweatpants.

You tell your partner, "I need time to write!" and then add the dialogue tag in your head: *"I need time to write!" she said, snapping the pencil she'd been holding in two..*

You're turned on more by foreshadowing than by foreplay.

Postage stamps are your idea of a thoughtful gift.

You relish reading a junky novel because every paragraph reminds you of how much better a writer you are than the author. At the same time, you are sick to your stomach: this hack at least got published.

Your wife tells you she backed the Jetta into a parked Ford Explorer, and all you can think about is how you would describe the thud of metal on metal.

You keep different journals for different moods.

You own the twenty-volume *Oxford English Dictionary* and *The Hypochondriac's Handbook*.

You keep a thesaurus in your purse or backpack.

Your proudest possession is a first edition of Strunk and White's *The Elements of Style*.

The fire department came
when you tried to burn
your 600-page manuscript
in a fireplace that didn't
work, either.

You'd write during the long rides up the ski lift if you could figure out a way to take off your goggles, put on your reading glasses, remove your gloves, and find a pen without dropping the poles or falling off the lift.

On the other hand, falling off the lift would make a great story.

You've started buying expensive Italian hardbound journals, just in case you're published posthumously.

You're sure your editor reads your writing aloud to his coworkers, all of them doubling over with laughter at how bad it is.

At work you practice turning off your computer screen quickly, for when someone glances over your shoulder at what you're writing.

You spot an office supply store and
have to force yourself to keep driving.

You modestly hand your income tax
return to those who think you can't
write fiction.

You sweat over your Christmas letter as
if it were *Remembrance of Things Past*.

You squeeze a paragraph into the
memo line on a personal check.

You keep a list of words and phrases you like: *"Italian summertime. Fester. Chiaroscuro."*

You hire a babysitter to watch your kid so you can go to your office and write about how much you love him.

You assess every person you meet as either good or poor character material.

You wonder whether your ongoing feud
with the florist down the street would
be best captured in a personal essay,
a short story, a novella, a three-book
epic, or a movie.

Your office memos start with an initiat-
ing incident and end with an epiphany.

Throwing out old files, you come across
a great piece and are delighted to realize you wrote it.

You scan your grocery receipt and mentally work all of the items into a narrative: *Disappointed to see the eggnog was sold out, she turned with mounting despair to the next item on her list, Swiss chard, and thought back to that autumn evening years ago . . .*

Sometimes you can no longer see the keyboard through your tears.

You spend an afternoon writing and
rewriting a breakup note in which you
say nothing about your feelings but
come up with some dazzling wordplay.
By the end, you can't remember why
you were so mad. You send the note
anyway, because who wants to waste
all those great lines?

You read the Bible looking for book titles.

You would rather read the label on an
oil painting than look at the painting.

Your pencils outlast their erasers.

You run out of room on Hallmark cards.

You read not for pleasure, but to find
out where the competition is.

You liked the book better than the movie.

You'd rather not think about that long, bleak period from your birth to the day you discovered reading.

Your heartbeat quickens whenever you enter a bookstore.

Despite anxiety, humiliation, and frustration, you can't stop writing, because you are doing exactly what you should be doing.

You pore over the "Contributors" page in your *New Yorker* magazine to see if any first-time authors were published that week.

Your surgeon had to take away the pen and notepad you were clutching on the operating table.

You'd write anything they let you write: horoscopes, greeting cards, catalog copy. You've even wondered how much fortune cookie writers make.

You tell the manager at your local hardware store that aisle four should say "Boys' Toys," not "Boy's Toys."

Your cat walks on your keyboard; you yell and butt your head at him but don't stop typing.

You read the dedications and acknowledgments in every new book to see if there's anyone you know.

You can take criticism
gracefully from anybody
but a relative, a friend,
an acquaintance, or a
stranger.

You refuse to get rid of any book you've
read, even the ones you hated, such as
The Bridges of Madison County.

You've been working on your memoir
so long that you have to keep changing
the ages of your kids.

You use a keyboard so much that
when you write with a pen, you make
typing errors, such as, "When I was
a samll child."

You go out in a snowstorm wearing a
T-shirt because it was summer when
you sat down to start your novel.

You have no idea who
Lindsay Lohan is.

No one will watch movies with you
anymore because you critique the
screenplay aloud.

You keep a notebook under your pillow.

You didn't notice a total eclipse of
the sun.

If you're not writing, you
do something crazy, such as
invest in uranium or weave
a room-size tapestry.

You're writing a detective novel, so you call six tailors to ask if it's possible to calculate the height of a man by the inseam of his pants.

You cry easily.

A dog barking two blocks away can
drive you nuts.

You know it takes a long time to write
something that appears dashed off.

You get a book idea while washing
the dishes.

You can't pay your electric bill because you scrawled notes for a new scene in chapter three on it.

You think of eavesdropping as research.

The back of your hand says, "What if the sister-in-law got pregnant by her boss?"

You write
what only
you could
write.

You pick up your fifteen-year-old at a police station and, even through your tears, you note ironic details such as the vending machine in the lobby flashing "Have A Nice Day" in red digital letters.

You cheerfully publish secrets that you have not gotten around to sharing with your own husband.

Not writing makes you depressed.

Friends hide car keys and sharp
objects from you when you're in the
middle of a writing project.

You try to concentrate on an e-mail
from your editor and find yourself
thinking instead about how the petals
from a flowering apple tree outside
have arranged themselves.

Preparing breakfast, you find yourself thinking, *Now she strides swiftly to the cupboard and grabs the sugar bowl.*

You have a journal for every year of your life, starting at age six.

The café won't lend you pens anymore.

You revise an e-mail ten times before pressing Send, and then spend the next hour frantically calling the computer guy to ask how you can get it back for just one more teensy change.

Your promise to yourself to quit writing and get a real job runs to fifteen single-spaced pages printed front and back, with a four-page addendum.

Lines form behind you in public bathrooms as you critique and correct stall scrawl.

You fell in love with a man because he used "frisson" and "palimpsest" in cocktail-party conversation.

You broke up with a woman because you didn't see a future with someone who pronounces "Proust" as rhyming with "soused."

Your first response on receiving a "Dear Jane" (or John) letter is not outrage at the content, but an urge to edit it for clarity and grammar.

A guy in the parking lot yells, "Hey, move your car, willya," and you wonder how you would punctuate what he said: exclamation point or question mark?

Sure, you read the fine print, but you think it needs work.

You use em-dashes and semicolons in your text messages.

In college you picked one word each
semester to work into every assignment
you turned in, regardless of subject or
topic: "myriad," "panoply," "tapestry,"
"unconscionable," "ontology," "artichoke."

You think people who eat alphabet soup
are barbarians.

Writing is the only thing that makes
you happy, and you hate writing.

A new ream of blank paper can bring on an anxiety attack.

You had to scrawl "Writing is fun!" on your computer with a Sharpie.

You catch yourself patting your laptop when you close it down.

You forgot your bathing suit on a trip to Tahiti, but remembered your laptop.

You know it's a mug's game—the odds
of getting published don't favor you—
but you don't care.

You are convinced that your editor,
agent, publicist, and the entire publish-
ing industry are in cahoots to thwart
your genius.

Your 600-page memoir's in your desk,
ready to be published the minute your
last relative dies.

At parties, you check out the bookshelves the way other people snoop through medicine cabinets.

You're proud of a rejection letter from *The New Yorker*.

Sometimes you think in an English accent.

You tell people you're a writer and then add, "But not a very good one." You know that a show of modesty gives you credibility.

You reread your own love scenes for
inspiration in the bedroom.

☺

You're from Nebraska, but you can't help
feeling that you are somehow British.

♨

You have a file on each member of
your family.

Your grocery list reads:
"Creamy fresh milk,
grapes picked glistening
from the vine, lettuce
pulled from the earth by
strong brown arms . . ."

Writing scares you.

You write in restaurants.

You watch a movie that doesn't make sense and imagine the screenwriter thinking, *Nobody will notice that.*

You can write no matter what mood
you're in.

You took time off to write a novel
and found so many ways to avoid the
actual writing that now you know how
to reglaze a window; cook a perfect
French cassoulet; change the car's oil,
belts, hoses, tires, and bulb; and fix
pilot lights.

You have lost friends because of what
you wrote.

Your spices are alphabetized.

You can work alone in a room for a year.

As you're staring out the window,
you're working.

People are disappointed when they
meet you in person.

You turn your worst moments
into money.

You're still steamed about the measly B-minus your daughter got on the *Great Expectations* paper you helped her with.

You know that thirty-nine drafts aren't enough and forty-two are too many.

You can't kill yourself because the suicide note isn't right. Should it be "I hate my life" or "I loathe my life"? Or should you go for the great exit line "I have decided to quit smoking"?

If they paid you to not write, you would write anyway.

You've stopped using the word "but"
after you answer, "Yes, I'm a writer."

You'd rather visit Stratford-upon-Avon
than the pyramids of Egypt.

You envy Oscar Wilde his last words,
"Either this wallpaper goes or I do."

Even as you kneel grieving in the
road where your beloved dog has been
injured by a bus, you memorize the way
your body bends forward, as it occurs
to you that a character in your novel
could have his dog struck by a bus.

Just as the Plains Indians used every
part of the buffalo, you use everything
that happens to you in your writing.

You keep a bad job because it's good
material.

You force yourself to have dinner alone
in a restaurant just so you can write
about it.

You're afraid you're too
well-adjusted to be a real
writer, so you wear black
to compensate.

You hold your cell phone up at intersections to record the sound of Italian motorbikes for that scene you're writing about a love affair on Capri.

Mr. Knightley was your first crush.

You were nine when you started writing poems, twelve when you moved on to tragic stories.

You carry around a pack of Gauloises
even though you don't smoke. They just
make you look so poetic.

You don't want to write, but you want
to have written.

Everything you write falls short of
what is in your head.

You have a working spouse who brings
in the rent.

A friend timidly asks if you really need
the scene where the uncle loses his
umbrella, and you realize you don't
like that friend as much as you thought
you did.

You know
that bracing
self-confidence
in a writer
is a sign
of psychic
instability.

You can do without anything but praise.

You believe that only words can create
a world that makes sense.

You head for the bookstore when something goes wrong in your life.

You dreamed that Dave Eggers got
in bed with you. The next night, you
dreamed it was Jhumpa Lahiri.

You refer to your law career as your
"day job."

You have an agreement with the post office: once you have sent an envelope off, you can't go down there to beg for it back so you can make more changes.

Some days it feels as if writing is the only thing that keeps you sane.

You get home to realize you bought the printer cartridge you went out for, but forgot the milk.

You would have to write even if you knew for sure that no one would ever read a word of it.

You don't remember events from your past anymore; you remember what you wrote.

You watch your husband intently while he reads your pieces. When he laughs, you say, "What part are you up to?"

You secretly hope it will rain on your vacation.

You like filling out forms, and you always ask for extra time.

You realize one day you've become a print glutton. You read half a dozen works simultaneously and treat each new book as the possible true Holy Grail. You feel so passionate about certain titles that you find yourself unable to speak about them at all.

The sight of a coffee mug full of pens, markers, and pencils energizes you more than coffee itself.

You have a scrapbook of thank-you notes from writers to whom you've written gushing letters.

You keep certain books—
The Letters of Vincent van Gogh, Swann's Way, The Poems of Richard Wilbur, A Death in the Family—near to hand at all times.

You're at the movies when you get an idea for your novel, so you scratch it into the bottom of your popcorn cup with a car key.

Your mom says, "Now I'm ironing the placket" and you're standing beside her thinking, *Placket. Good word.*

You wonder which is a funnier word for a mineral, "feldspar" or "potash."

You can almost get high on the smell of a freshly sharpened pencil.

You don't know what you think until you see what you wrote.

No one knew about your husband's paralyzing arachnophobia until you outed him in your book.

You read a book with a pen in your hand and scan the newspaper holding scissors.

You are furious that you were born too late to go west in a covered wagon.

Your driver's license reads,
Eyes: shifty. Hair: windswept.

You've wanted to be a writer since
Mrs. Burnett tacked your Christmas
poem to the bulletin board in the
third grade.

You keep a legal pad in the front seat
of your car so that you can write on it
while driving.

You copy and paste the e-mails you
write into your journal.

You excuse yourself from an intimate moment with your mate to run to the bathroom and jot down the details in the notebook you keep in a drawer there.

Each new word is like a present. When your new love interrupts an argument to say "I don't want a disquisition," you are entranced. You've heard of "inquisition," but not "disquisition." You're so happy with your shiny new word that you don't hear him slam the door on his way out.

As the handlebar breaks on your bike, you have the first line written before your head hits the pavement.

You wish they gave you more room on your tax returns. It's important for your accountant to understand the melancholy mood you were in that rainy day when your boyfriend hadn't called and you bought the Mont Blanc pen set to cheer yourself up.

You're answering the "family medical history" question at the doctor's office, and you list that your uncle was addicted to Billie Holiday records, your grandmother was exactly as old as penicillin, and your father suffered from an ailment you describe as "chronically unsupportive of my talents."

You fire a "How could you charge me these fees?" letter to your bank. The bank calls to say they are dropping the fees because they liked the note so much.

You editor calls to say he needs a book with 250 casserole recipes in six months. Instead of telling him he's insane, you say, "I'd better get busy."

You signed high school yearbooks in iambic pentameter.

You like every-
thing about
writing except
the paperwork.

You are depressed—you're sure you've gained thirty-five pounds since yesterday. Yet somehow, scribbling away at your desk for an hour or two makes you feel as if you've lost enough weight to get dressed and maybe, *maybe* even leave the house.

You get carpal tunnel syndrome from too much typing, so you switch the next day to voice recognition software.

You have written so much about your parents, and taken so many liberties along the way, that you can no longer tell what happened from what you made up. Did your parents really own a puppet theater?

You are weaning yourself off adverbs
the way others wean themselves
off chocolate.

God forbid you'd ever need to, but
if called upon, you would write a
killer eulogy.

Your work clothes are a ratty bathrobe and duck slippers, and your commute is ten seconds—thirty if you stop at the bathroom.

Some people have the Bible, some the Koran; you have *The Chicago Manual of Style.*

You look up "parsimony" in the dictionary and don't stop reading till you hit "psalm."

You buy a book called *You Know You're a Writer When ...*

Adair Lara, author of the charming and popular *Normal is Just a Setting on the Dryer* and many other books, was a reporter and columnist for the *San Francisco Chronicle* for nineteen years before becoming a full-time author. She is also the founder of Matchwriters.com, a Web site where writers can meet other writers.